# THE PRAYING ATHLETE™
# QUOTE BOOK

## VOL 5

### STAYING
MOTIVATED

Published by The Core Media Group, Inc., P.O. Box 2037, Indian Trail, NC 28079.

Cover & Interior Design: Ashlyn Helms

Printed in the United States of America.

# CHECK OUT OUR

## THE PRAYING ATHLETE™
## PHOTOGRAPHY
## QUOTE BOOKS

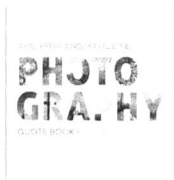

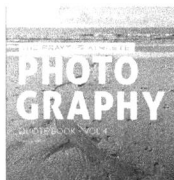
*The Praying Athlete Photography Quote Book*s celebrate God's glory and magnificence through His creation. They contain photos taken by Robert B. Walker, paired with his words of wisdom, motivation, and inspiration.

www.ingramcontent.com/pod-product-compliance
Lightning Source LLC
Chambersburg PA
CBHW060042040426
42331CB00032B/2196

# VOL 5 STAYING MOTIVATED

Today was gifted to you.
Now choose what to do with
the gift of today. You can put
it away and not open the gift
of today, or you can unwrap
your day and put all your
talents to use to make
tomorrow an even better day.

Going places takes energy
and progress every second to
get to where you want to be.
Always remember to keep
pressing when it gets tough.
You WILL get there.

How do you get from
good to great?
Push the good to the side and
always focus on being great.
Greatness will arrive.

Are you a leader?
How do you know
if you have never defined
what a leader is?

Go out and achieve
the impossible.

I'm not finished with what
God has challenged me to
accomplish in my life.

Why sweat the moment when
the One you know is there
with you in the moment?

Do your circumstances
intimidate you? Pray and let
God give you the wisdom to
be an overcomer!

Do what you need to do to
dream again.
Fill the visions of your life and
dream on.

In despair, there is hope
around the corner.

Be that hope so that
others can find it.

Building your own success
is much more important
than someone handing
you success.

Today, do something
to be something
**UNBELIEVABLE.**

You cannot become what you
need to be and what
God wants you to be if you
remain where you are.
Strive to do more.

What time is it in your life?
Always be engaged in a
season of growth, finding
ways to study, read, and grow
your circle of influence.

What is your ground speed?
How quickly do you pursue
your goals and plans?
A slow ground speed will not
take you anywhere fast.
It is a big world out there with
many goals to achieve.
Increase your ground
speed today.

Today is the first day of your new life. God created you and me to have a fresh start every day.

The storms may gather and
the wind may blow but I know
the sun will always show
through the darkness of life.

If you look closely, help is
always on the way.
Sometimes, it is hard to see,
but God always delivers.

New opportunities bring
new ways to rise to the
top of your career.
So, the stress you feel is not
real, but the enthusiasm
for what is ahead is what
keeps you on top.

Be on the front lines and lead.

People will try to wipe you away
and discount who you are and
say things that will hurt you. But
stand tall and fly away to those
you know care and love you.

Grab life and fill it with love,
joy, peace and happiness.

God gave you a special
talent to elevate Him and to
bless you and your family.
Through this gift he has given
you, it will build a platform
for a stronger and deeper
faith as you rely on God
and not yourself.
Now, embrace your talent.
All the confidence is already
within you, so ACTIVATE it!

Renewable energy is a hot
topic today. How can you help
others renew their interest,
energy, and zeal for life?

Have you ever been on a balance beam? Have you seen the routines by some of the best during the Olympics? Balance in life is very challenging. Be prepared for the fall—it will happen. Even the best fall. It is the getting back up that requires the discipline and self-motivation to conquer any self-doubt. The victory is getting back up!

**The tongue is such a powerful tool. Use it to give words of affirmation every day.**

Why do people drive slow in the fast lane? Step aside, and let us move. We are trying to make something happen.

A goal in life should be to
empower people and give
away whatever knowledge
you have to them.

So many times, we as athletes put undue pressure on our talents. When we do this, we play robotically and that limits our potential. Play with zeal and passion for the game you love, and you will leave anxiety behind.
You will then surpass what was possible and begin reaching what others thought was impossible.

## THOUGHTS & REFLECTIONS

_____

_____

_____

_____

_____

_____

_____

_____

_____

_____

_____

_____

_____

_____

_____

_____

_____

_____

_____

_____

_____

_____

_____

_____

_____

_____

_____

_____

_____

_____

_____

---
---
---
---
---
---
---
---
---
---
---
---
---
---
---
---
---
---

_____

_____

_____

_____

_____

_____

_____

_____

_____

_____

_____

_____

_____

_____

_____

_____

_____

## MY QUOTES

_____
_____
_____
_____
_____
_____
_____
_____
_____
_____
_____
_____
_____
_____
_____
_____

_____

_____

_____

_____

_____

_____

_____

_____

_____

_____

_____

_____

_____

_____

_____

_____

_____

_____

# ACKNOWLEDGEMENTS

I want to acknowledge and say thank you to all those that helped with this project:

Nadia Guy
Ashlyn Helms
My Mom & Dad

All of my NFL Clients, current and former, that have encouraged me to share these words with others.

# ABOUT
# TPA

The Praying Athlete is a movement that creates an organic culture of prayer through an uplifting community and authentic conversation.

For more information, visit our website **www.theprayingathlete.com**.

Follow us on social media.

 @ThePrayingAthlete

 @Praying_Athlete

 @ThePrayingAthlete

# COLLECT ALL

# 8 VOL.

Our first volume of *The Praying Athlete Quote Book* addresses the topic of playing the game. Quotes and thoughts from Robert B. Walker, paired with Scripture from God's Word, allow readers to get a good idea about what playing a good game looks like.

Our second volume of *The Praying Athlete Quote Book* addresses the topic of teamwork. Quotes and thoughts from Robert B. Walker, paired with Scripture from God's Word, allow readers to understand what it means to be a good teammate and surround yourself with people who lift you up.

Our third volume of *The Praying Athlete Quote Book* addresses the topic of growth & preparation for the future. Quotes and thoughts from Robert B. Walker, paired with Scripture from God's Word, allow readers to know that even though the future is uncertain, there is a plan and purpose for everyone.

Our fourth volume of *The Praying Athlete Quote Book* addresses the topic of keeping the right mentality. Quotes and thoughts from Robert B. Walker allow readers to understand how staying in the right mindset can improve overall performance.

Our fifth volume of *The Praying Athlete Quote Book* addresses the topic of staying motivated. Quotes and thoughts from Robert B. Walker allow readers to become motivated to accomplish their goals, even when they feel they are not up to the task.

Our sixth volume of *The Praying Athlete Quote Book* addresses the topic of personal accountability. Quotes and thoughts from Robert B. Walker allow readers to think about how they can better themselves. Whether its ending a bad habit or saying no to anything that may hurt themselves or others, staying accountable will benefit one's character and performance.

Our seventh volume of *The Praying Athlete Quote Book* addresses the topic of living life. This volume is the first part in a two part living life series. Quotes and thoughts from Robert B. Walker give readers a better understanding of how to live life to the fullest.

Our eighth volume of *The Praying Athlete Quote Book* addresses the topic of living life. This volume is the second part in a two part living life series. Quotes and thoughts from Robert B. Walker give readers a better understanding of how to live life to the fullest.